THE HE...

UNVEILED

Discover The Secrets To Achieving Lasting Mental Health

By

Serenity Muse

Copyright © 2024 by Serenity Muse

All rights reserved. No part of this publication may be reproduced, distributed, or transmitted in any form or by any means, including photocopying, recording, or other electronic or mechanical methods, without the prior written permission of the publisher, except in the case of brief quotations embodied in critical reviews and certain other noncommercial uses permitted by copyright law.

This book is a work of nonfiction. The views, opinions, and strategies expressed are those of the author and do not necessarily reflect the official policy or position of any other individual, agency, organization, or company.

ABOUT THE AUTHOR

Serenity Muse's Journey and Philosophy

Serenity Muse is a seasoned mental health professional with over three decades of experience dedicated to helping individuals achieve happiness and fulfillment in their lives. With a background in psychology and a passion for holistic well-being, Serenity Muse has touched the lives of many through counseling, coaching, and educational workshops aimed at promoting emotional resilience and personal growth.

Throughout her career, Serenity Muse has embraced a philosophy centered on the transformative power of self-awareness, compassion, and intentional living. Her approach integrates evidence-based practices from positive psychology, mindfulness, and cognitive-behavioral techniques to empower individuals in overcoming challenges, embracing change, and fostering meaningful connections.

Serenity Muse's journey began with a deep-seated commitment to understanding the complexities of human emotions and behaviors. This led her to explore various modalities and therapeutic approaches that resonate with her belief in the inherent potential for growth and healing within each person. Her work emphasizes the importance of self-care, self-compassion, and cultivating resilience as pillars of well-being in navigating life's transitions and challenges.

Contact Information and Future Projects

For more information about Serenity Muse, upcoming projects, or to connect directly:

Email: serenitymuse360@gmail.com

Website: www.serenitymuse.org

Future projects from Serenity Muse include expanding her outreach through:

- Books and Publications: Continuing to explore topics related to happiness, personal growth, and resilience through written works that inspire and empower readers.

- Workshops and Seminars: Offering interactive workshops and seminars designed to enhance emotional well-being, mindfulness practices, and effective communication skills.

- Community Engagement: Collaborating with organizations and communities to promote mental health awareness, holistic wellness, and strategies for building supportive relationships.

Serenity Muse remains dedicated to supporting individuals on their journey toward happiness and fulfillment, advocating for self-discovery, authenticity, and the pursuit of a meaningful life.

TABLE OF CONTENTS

INTRODUCTION: THE JOURNEY INTO THE HUMAN MIND 7

   Understanding Mental Health 7

CHAPTER 1: FOUNDATIONS OF MENTAL HEALTH 11

   Defining Mental Health 11

CHAPTER 2: THE SCIENCE OF THE BRAIN 17

   Brain Structure and Function 17

CHAPTER 3: RECOGNIZING MENTAL HEALTH DISORDERS 23

   Anxiety Disorders 23

CHAPTER 4: FACTORS INFLUENCING MENTAL HEALTH 31

   Genetic Predispositions 31

CHAPTER 5: STRATEGIES FOR MENTAL WELLBEING 38

   Mindfulness And Meditation 38

CHAPTER 6: THE ROLE OF THERAPY AND COUNSELING 46

   Types Of Therapy 46

CHAPTER 7: COPING MECHANISMS AND RESILIENCE 54

   Stress Management Techniques 54

CHAPTER 8: THE IMPACT OF RELATIONSHIPS 61

    Healthy Relationships and Mental Health 61

CHAPTER 9: MENTAL HEALTH IN DIFFERENT LIFE STAGES 70

    Childhood And Adolescence 70

CHAPTER 10: MODERN CHALLENGES TO MENTAL HEALTH 78

    Technology And Mental Health 78

CHAPTER 11: CREATING A MENTAL HEALTH PLAN 86

    Setting Mental Health Goals 86

CHAPTER 12: RESOURCES AND FURTHER READING 94

    Books, Websites, And Organizations 94

CONCLUSION: CONTINUING THE JOURNEY 102

    Summarizing Key Points 102

INTRODUCTION: THE JOURNEY INTO THE HUMAN MIND

Understanding Mental Health

In today's fast-paced, interconnected world, mental health has become a crucial aspect of our overall well-being. Yet, it remains one of the most misunderstood and stigmatized areas of health. What exactly is mental health? At its core, mental health encompasses our emotional, psychological, and social well-being. It affects how we think, feel, and act. It also helps determine how we handle stress, relate to others, and make choices. Mental health is not merely the absence of mental illness but a state of well-being in which an individual realizes their own potential, can cope with the normal stresses of life, can work productively, and is able to make a contribution to their community.

Mental health influences every aspect of our lives. It dictates how we form relationships, perform at work or school, and interact within our communities. Despite its importance, many people fail to recognize the signs of mental health issues or are reluctant to seek help due to the stigma associated with it. This book aims to break down these barriers by providing a practical and comprehensive guide to understanding the human mind and promoting mental well-being.

Importance of Mental Wellbeing

The importance of mental well-being cannot be overstated. It is integral to our overall health, just as vital as physical health. Good mental health enables us to enjoy life, maintain a balance between life's activities and efforts to achieve psychological resilience. When we are mentally healthy, we can more effectively manage stress, build and sustain relationships, and recover from setbacks.

Mental well-being is essential for fostering a productive and fulfilling life. It allows us to adapt to changes, cope with adversity, and navigate the complexities of modern life. Mental health problems can impair these abilities, leading to diminished functioning and quality of life. The economic impact of poor mental health is also significant, affecting productivity, increasing healthcare costs, and straining social services.

In this book, we will delve into the various factors that affect mental health, from biological and psychological to social and environmental influences. We will explore practical strategies for maintaining and improving mental well-being, and provide tools and resources to help you and those around you thrive.

How to Use This Guide

"Decoding Mental Health: A Practical Guide to Understanding the Human Mind - Unveiling the Secrets to Mental Wellbeing" is designed to be a comprehensive resource for anyone seeking to improve their mental health or support others in their mental health journey. Whether you are a student, a professional, a caregiver, or simply someone interested in better understanding the complexities of the human mind, this book offers valuable insights and practical advice.

Each chapter is structured to provide a thorough understanding of key concepts related to mental health. We begin with the foundational aspects of mental health, exploring what it is and why it matters. From there, we delve into the science of the brain, identifying how its structure and function influence mental well-being. We also cover a range of mental health disorders, examining their symptoms, causes, and treatment options.

The book then shifts focus to the various factors that influence mental health, including genetics, environment, and lifestyle choices. We provide practical strategies for enhancing mental well-being, from mindfulness and physical activity to nutrition and therapy. Additionally, we discuss the importance of relationships and social support, and how different stages of life present unique mental health challenges.

To maximize the benefits of this guide, we encourage you to approach it with an open mind and a willingness to explore new ideas and practices. Mental health is a deeply personal journey, and what works for one person may not work for another. Therefore, we present a range of options and encourage you to experiment with different strategies to find what best suits your needs.

Throughout the book, you will find exercises, tips, and real-life examples to help you apply the concepts discussed. We also include a section on creating a personalized mental health plan, setting achievable goals, and tracking your progress. Our aim is to empower you with the knowledge and tools necessary to take charge of your mental health and enhance your overall well-being.

As you embark on this journey into the human mind, remember that seeking help is a sign of strength, not weakness. Mental health is a vital component of a healthy, fulfilling life, and by prioritizing it, you are taking an essential step towards achieving your fullest potential. Welcome to a transformative journey towards understanding and nurturing your mental well-being.

CHAPTER 1: FOUNDATIONS OF MENTAL HEALTH

Defining Mental Health

Mental health is a multifaceted concept that encompasses our emotional, psychological, and social well-being. It influences how we think, feel, and behave in our daily lives. Good mental health allows us to cope with the inevitable stresses of life, work productively, and contribute to our communities. But what exactly constitutes mental health?

Mental health is not simply the absence of mental illness. It involves a state of balance in which an individual can realize their own abilities, handle normal stresses, work productively, and contribute to their community. It is a dynamic state, fluctuating over time in response to personal and external factors. Understanding mental health as a continuum rather than a binary state helps us recognize that everyone falls somewhere along the spectrum and that our position can change based on life circumstances, environment, and personal choices.

A comprehensive definition of mental health includes:
- Emotional well-being: The ability to identify, express, and manage a range of emotions.

- Psychological well-being: The capacity to think clearly, reason, and solve problems.
- Social well-being: The ability to form and maintain relationships and interact positively with others.

By appreciating these dimensions, we can better understand the complexity of mental health and the various factors that contribute to it.

The Mind-Body Connection

The connection between mind and body is a foundational concept in understanding mental health. This relationship is bidirectional, meaning that our mental state can influence our physical health and vice versa. For instance, chronic stress can lead to physical symptoms such as headaches, high blood pressure, and a weakened immune system. Conversely, physical health problems can impact our mental well-being, leading to feelings of anxiety, depression, or stress.

One of the most significant aspects of the mind-body connection is the role of stress. Stress triggers a cascade of hormonal responses in the body, primarily involving the hypothalamic-pituitary-adrenal (HPA) axis. This results in the release of cortisol, the body's primary stress hormone, which prepares us to respond to perceived threats. While short-term stress can be beneficial, chronic stress can lead to detrimental effects on both mental and physical health, contributing to conditions such as anxiety, depression, heart disease, and diabetes.

Another critical element of the mind-body connection is the impact of lifestyle choices on mental health. Regular physical activity, for example, has been shown to improve mood and reduce symptoms of depression and anxiety. Exercise stimulates the release of endorphins, which are natural mood lifters. Similarly, nutrition plays a crucial role in mental health. A diet rich in fruits, vegetables, whole grains, and lean proteins can support brain function and promote emotional stability.

Sleep is another vital component of the mind-body connection. Poor sleep can impair cognitive function, increase irritability, and exacerbate mental health issues. Conversely, good sleep hygiene can enhance mood, improve concentration, and foster emotional resilience. Practices such as maintaining a regular sleep schedule, creating a restful sleep environment, and limiting exposure to screens before bedtime can significantly improve sleep quality and, by extension, mental health.

Understanding the mind-body connection empowers us to make informed choices that support both our physical and mental well-being. By adopting healthy lifestyle habits, we can create a foundation for enduring mental health.

Common Mental Health Myths

Despite growing awareness, mental health is still surrounded by myths and misconceptions that can prevent people from seeking help or understanding the true nature of mental health issues. Debunking these myths is essential for fostering a more informed and compassionate society.

Myth 1: Mental health problems are rare.

In reality, mental health issues are incredibly common. According to the World Health Organization, one in four people will experience a mental health condition at some point in their lives. Mental health issues do not discriminate and can affect anyone, regardless of age, gender, socioeconomic status, or background.

Myth 2: Mental health problems are a sign of weakness.

This myth perpetuates the harmful stigma surrounding mental health. Mental health issues are not a result of personal weakness or character flaws. They are complex conditions influenced by a variety of factors, including genetics, environment, and life experiences. Seeking help for mental health problems is a sign of strength and self-awareness, not weakness.

Myth 3: People with mental health conditions are dangerous.

The portrayal of individuals with mental health issues as dangerous is largely unfounded and contributes to fear and discrimination. The vast majority of people with mental health conditions are not violent. In fact, they are more likely to be victims of violence than perpetrators. It is essential to challenge these stereotypes and promote a more accurate understanding of mental health.

Myth 4: Mental health issues will go away on their own.

Ignoring mental health problems can lead to worsening symptoms and decreased quality of life. Like physical health conditions, mental health issues often require professional treatment and support. Early intervention can significantly improve outcomes and help individuals manage their symptoms more effectively.

Myth 5: Therapy is only for people with severe mental health problems.

Therapy can benefit anyone, regardless of the severity of their mental health issues. It provides a safe space to explore thoughts, feelings, and behaviors, and develop coping strategies. Whether dealing with everyday stress, relationship challenges, or more severe conditions, therapy can be a valuable tool for personal growth and well-being.

Implementing the Foundations

Understanding these foundational aspects of mental health sets the stage for a deeper exploration into the human mind. By recognizing the complexity of mental health, acknowledging the mind-body connection, and dispelling common myths, we can create a more informed and supportive environment for ourselves and others.

To implement these concepts in your daily life, start by assessing your own mental health. Reflect on your emotional, psychological, and social well-being. Identify areas where you may need support or improvement. Incorporate healthy lifestyle habits such as regular exercise, balanced nutrition, and good sleep hygiene into your routine. Stay informed and challenge misconceptions about mental health, both in your own thinking and in conversations with others.

Remember, mental health is a journey, not a destination. By building a strong foundation of understanding, you are taking the first steps toward a healthier, more fulfilling life. The chapters that follow will delve deeper into the science of the brain, the recognition and management of mental health disorders, and practical strategies for enhancing mental well-being. Embrace this journey with an open mind and a commitment to nurturing your mental health.

CHAPTER 2: THE SCIENCE OF THE BRAIN

Brain Structure and Function

The human brain is a marvel of biological engineering, responsible for everything we think, feel, and do. Understanding its structure and function is crucial to grasping how mental health and brain health are intertwined.

The brain is composed of three main parts: the cerebrum, the cerebellum, and the brainstem.

Cerebrum: The largest part of the brain, the cerebrum, is divided into two hemispheres (left and right) and is responsible for higher brain functions such as thought, action, and personality. Each hemisphere controls the opposite side of the body. The cerebrum is further divided into four lobes:

- **Frontal Lobe:** Associated with reasoning, planning, parts of speech, movement, emotions, and problem-solving.

- **Parietal Lobe:** Processes sensory information such as touch, temperature, and pain.
- **Occipital Lobe:** Responsible for visual processing.
- **Temporal Lobe:** Involved in perception and recognition of auditory stimuli, memory, and speech.

Cerebellum: Located under the cerebrum, the cerebellum controls motor functions. It helps with balance, coordination, and fine-tuning of movements.

Brainstem: The brainstem connects the brain to the spinal cord and regulates vital functions such as heart rate, breathing, and sleep cycles.

Neurotransmitters and Their Role

Neurotransmitters are the brain's chemical messengers. They transmit signals across synapses from one neuron to another, influencing every aspect of brain function. Here are some key neurotransmitters and their roles:

Dopamine: Often called the "feel-good" neurotransmitter, dopamine is crucial for pleasure, reward, and motivation. It also plays a role in movement and emotional responses. Abnormal levels of dopamine are linked to conditions like Parkinson's disease, schizophrenia, and addiction.

Serotonin: This neurotransmitter contributes to well-being and happiness. It helps regulate mood, appetite, and sleep. Low levels of serotonin are commonly associated with depression and anxiety.

Norepinephrine: Involved in the body's "fight or flight" response, norepinephrine increases alertness and arousal. It also helps regulate mood. Imbalances can contribute to anxiety and mood disorders.

GABA (Gamma-Aminobutyric Acid): GABA is an inhibitory neurotransmitter that reduces neuronal excitability, promoting relaxation and reducing anxiety. Low levels of GABA are associated with anxiety disorders.

Glutamate: The most abundant excitatory neurotransmitter in the brain, glutamate is involved in cognitive functions such as learning and memory. Excessive glutamate activity is linked to neurodegenerative diseases like Alzheimer's.

Acetylcholine: This neurotransmitter plays a crucial role in muscle action, learning, and memory. Dysfunction in acetylcholine signaling is associated with Alzheimer's disease.

Understanding the roles of these neurotransmitters helps us comprehend how chemical imbalances can affect mood, behavior, and overall mental health. Treatments for mental health disorders often aim to restore the balance of neurotransmitters.

The Brain's Plasticity

One of the most remarkable features of the brain is its plasticity, or neuroplasticity, which refers to the brain's ability to change and adapt as a result of experience. This adaptability occurs at multiple levels, from cellular changes due to learning to large-scale cortical remapping in response to injury.

Synaptic Plasticity: This involves changes in the strength of connections between neurons. Synaptic plasticity is essential for learning and memory. For instance, when we learn a new skill, the synaptic connections involved in that skill become stronger and more efficient.

Structural Plasticity: The brain can also change its physical structure in response to learning, experience, or injury. This includes the growth of new neurons (neurogenesis) and the formation of new synapses.

Functional Plasticity: This refers to the brain's ability to move functions from damaged areas to undamaged areas. For example, if one part of the brain is damaged, another part can sometimes take over the lost function. This ability is particularly important in recovery from brain injuries such as strokes.

Environmental Influence: The brain's plasticity is heavily influenced by our environment and experiences. Enriching environments with stimuli such as learning opportunities, social interactions, and physical activity can enhance neuroplasticity. Conversely, stressful or impoverished environments can hinder it.

Practical Applications: Understanding neuroplasticity has practical implications for mental health. It underscores the importance of engaging in activities that promote brain health, such as continuous learning, physical exercise, and stress management techniques like mindfulness and meditation. Therapies such as cognitive-behavioral therapy (CBT) leverage the brain's plasticity to help individuals reframe negative thought patterns and develop healthier behaviors.

Implementing the Science of the Brain

To harness the knowledge of brain structure, neurotransmitters, and neuroplasticity for better mental health, consider the following steps:

1. **Engage in Regular Physical Activity:** Exercise increases blood flow to the brain and promotes the release of

beneficial neurotransmitters such as endorphins, dopamine, and serotonin.
2. **Practice Mindfulness and Meditation:** These practices can enhance neuroplasticity, reduce stress, and improve emotional regulation.
3. **Maintain a Balanced Diet:** A diet rich in omega-3 fatty acids, antioxidants, and vitamins supports brain health and neurotransmitter function.
4. **Prioritize Sleep:** Good sleep hygiene is essential for cognitive function and emotional stability. Aim for 7-9 hours of quality sleep per night.
5. **Continuous Learning:** Challenge your brain with new activities and learning opportunities to promote synaptic plasticity.
6. **Seek Professional Help:** If you experience persistent mental health issues, consult a healthcare provider. Treatments such as medication and therapy can help restore neurotransmitter balance and promote neuroplasticity.

By understanding the science of the brain, we can take proactive steps to enhance our mental well-being and harness the brain's incredible capacity for change and adaptation. In the chapters that follow, we will explore specific mental health disorders, their treatment options, and additional strategies for maintaining and improving mental health. Embrace this journey with the knowledge that your brain is a dynamic and adaptable organ and capable of growth.

CHAPTER 3: RECOGNIZING MENTAL HEALTH DISORDERS

Anxiety Disorders

Anxiety disorders are among the most common mental health conditions, characterized by excessive fear or worry. While anxiety is a normal response to stress, it becomes a disorder when it interferes with daily life. There are several types of anxiety disorders, each with unique features.

Generalized Anxiety Disorder (GAD): Individuals with GAD experience persistent and excessive worry about various aspects of life, such as work, health, or personal relationships. This worry is difficult to control and often comes with physical symptoms like restlessness, fatigue, difficulty concentrating, irritability, muscle tension, and sleep disturbances.

Panic Disorder: Panic disorder is characterized by recurrent, unexpected panic attacks. These are sudden periods of intense fear or discomfort that reach a peak within minutes and are accompanied by physical symptoms such as heart palpitations, sweating, trembling, shortness of breath, and a fear of losing control or impending doom. The unpredictability of panic attacks often leads to significant anxiety about future attacks.

Social Anxiety Disorder (SAD): Also known as social phobia, SAD involves an intense fear of social situations where one might be judged or scrutinized by others. This fear can be so severe that it interferes with daily activities such as work, school, and relationships. People with SAD may avoid social interactions or endure them with great distress.

Specific Phobias: A specific phobia is an intense, irrational fear of a particular object or situation, such as heights, flying, spiders, or needles. This fear leads to avoidance behavior and can significantly impact a person's life.

Obsessive-Compulsive Disorder (OCD): OCD involves unwanted, intrusive thoughts (obsessions) and repetitive behaviors or mental acts (compulsions) performed to reduce anxiety. For example, a person with OCD might be obsessed with germs and engage in excessive hand washing.

Post-Traumatic Stress Disorder (PTSD): PTSD can develop after exposure to a traumatic event, such as a natural disaster, accident, or assault. Symptoms include flashbacks, nightmares, severe anxiety, and uncontrollable thoughts about the event.

Mood Disorders

Mood disorders primarily affect a person's emotional state and can significantly disrupt daily functioning. They include conditions such as depression and bipolar disorder.

Major Depressive Disorder (MDD): MDD is characterized by persistent feelings of sadness, hopelessness, and a lack of interest or pleasure in activities. Other symptoms include changes in appetite and weight, sleep disturbances, fatigue, difficulty concentrating, and thoughts of death or suicide. These symptoms must last for at least two weeks and represent a change from previous functioning.

Persistent Depressive Disorder (PDD): Also known as dysthymia, PDD involves a chronic, low-grade depression that lasts for at least two years. Individuals with PDD experience many of the same symptoms as those with MDD, but they are usually less severe.

Bipolar Disorder: Bipolar disorder involves mood swings that include emotional highs (mania or hypomania) and lows (depression). During manic episodes, individuals may feel euphoric, energetic, or unusually irritable. These episodes can involve risky behaviors, rapid speech, and decreased need for sleep. Depressive episodes, on the other hand, involve feelings of sadness, hopelessness, and loss of interest in activities. Bipolar disorder is divided into Bipolar I, characterized by full-blown manic episodes, and Bipolar II, characterized by hypomanic (less severe manic) episodes and depressive episodes.

Cyclothymic Disorder: This disorder involves periods of hypomanic symptoms and periods of depressive symptoms that are less severe than those required to diagnose bipolar disorder. These mood swings must occur for at least two years.

Personality Disorders

Personality disorders are enduring patterns of behavior, cognition, and inner experience that deviate markedly from the expectations of an individual's culture. These patterns are inflexible, pervasive, and lead to significant distress or impairment.

Borderline Personality Disorder (BPD): BPD is characterized by instability in moods, behavior, self-image, and functioning. Individuals with BPD often experience intense episodes of anger, depression, and anxiety that may last only hours or at most a day. They may have difficulty maintaining stable relationships and often engage in impulsive or self-destructive behaviors, such as substance abuse or self-harm.

Narcissistic Personality Disorder (NPD): Individuals with NPD have an inflated sense of their own importance, a deep need for excessive attention and admiration, and a lack of empathy for others. They often exploit relationships and can become easily angered or depressed if criticized.

Antisocial Personality Disorder (ASPD): ASPD is characterized by a long-term pattern of disregard for, or violation of, the rights of others. Individuals with ASPD may engage in deceitful, manipulative, or illegal activities and often lack remorse for their actions.

Avoidant Personality Disorder (AvPD): AvPD involves extreme social inhibition, feelings of inadequacy, and sensitivity to negative criticism and rejection. Individuals with AvPD often avoid social interactions despite a desire for close relationships.

Psychotic Disorders

Psychotic disorders involve distorted thinking and awareness. The most common psychotic disorder is schizophrenia, but others include schizoaffective disorder and brief psychotic disorder.

Schizophrenia: Schizophrenia is a chronic brain disorder that affects less than one percent of the U.S. population. It is characterized by episodes of psychosis, including hallucinations (hearing or seeing things that aren't there), delusions (false beliefs), disorganized thinking, and abnormal motor behavior. Negative symptoms, such as diminished emotional expression or lack of motivation, are also common.

Schizoaffective Disorder: This disorder includes symptoms of both schizophrenia and mood disorders (depression or bipolar disorder). Individuals experience psychotic symptoms such as hallucinations or delusions, along with mood disorder symptoms.

Brief Psychotic Disorder: This disorder involves short, sudden episodes of psychotic behavior, often in response to a stressful event. These episodes typically last less than a month, with full recovery usually occurring.

Implementing Recognition of Mental Health Disorders

Recognizing mental health disorders is the first step towards seeking appropriate treatment and support. Here are some practical steps to implement this knowledge:

1. **Educate Yourself and Others:** Awareness is key. Educate yourself about the symptoms and characteristics of different mental health disorders. Share this knowledge with friends, family, and colleagues to reduce stigma and promote understanding.

2. **Observe and Reflect:** Pay attention to your own mental health and the well-being of those around you. Notice changes in behavior, mood, or functioning that persist and impact daily life.

3. **Seek Professional Help:** If you or someone you know exhibits signs of a mental health disorder, consult a healthcare professional. Early intervention can significantly improve outcomes.

4. **Promote a Supportive Environment:** Create a supportive and non-judgmental environment where people feel comfortable discussing their mental health. Encourage open communication and offer support to those in need.

5. **Utilize Resources:** Make use of available resources such as mental health hotlines, support groups, and online information. These can provide additional support and guidance.

6. **Practice Self-Care:** Engage in activities that promote mental well-being, such as regular exercise, healthy eating, adequate sleep, and stress management techniques.

By understanding and recognizing the signs of mental health disorders, we can take proactive steps to address them, support those affected, and foster a more compassionate and informed society. In the following chapters, we will explore the factors influencing mental health, strategies for maintaining mental well-being, and the role of therapy and counseling in treatment and support. This journey towards understanding and improving mental health is ongoing and essential for leading a balanced and fulfilling life.

CHAPTER 4: FACTORS INFLUENCING MENTAL HEALTH

Genetic Predispositions

The role of genetics in mental health is profound, shaping our susceptibility to various mental health disorders. While genes alone do not determine our mental health outcomes, they provide a blueprint that can influence how we respond to environmental and lifestyle factors.

Genetic Inheritance: Mental health disorders can run in families, suggesting a hereditary component. For example, conditions such as depression, bipolar disorder, and schizophrenia have been shown to have a genetic link. Researchers have identified specific genes and genetic variations that are associated with an increased risk of these disorders. However, having a genetic predisposition does not guarantee that an individual will develop a mental health condition. It merely indicates a higher likelihood, which may or may not be realized depending on other factors.

Gene-Environment Interaction: Our genes interact with environmental factors in complex ways. This interaction can amplify or mitigate the risk of developing mental health disorders. For instance, a person with a genetic predisposition to depression may never experience depressive episodes if they are raised in a supportive and nurturing environment. Conversely, a person without such a predisposition might develop depression in response to severe stress or trauma. This interplay underscores the importance of considering both genetic and environmental factors in understanding mental health.

Epigenetics: Epigenetics studies how environmental factors can influence gene expression without altering the DNA sequence. Epigenetic changes can be triggered by various factors, including stress, diet, behavior, and toxins. These changes can affect how genes are turned on or off, potentially leading to mental health disorders. For example, chronic stress can lead to epigenetic modifications that affect the expression of genes involved in the stress response, increasing the risk of anxiety and depression.

Implementing Genetic Knowledge: Understanding genetic predispositions can help individuals take proactive steps to mitigate their risk of mental health disorders. This might include engaging in regular mental health check-ups, adopting stress-reduction techniques, and creating a supportive social network. Awareness of one's genetic background can also inform personalized treatment plans that consider genetic factors alongside other influences.

Environmental Factors

The environment in which we live, work, and grow has a significant impact on our mental health. Various environmental factors can either enhance mental well-being or contribute to mental health issues.

Childhood Experiences: Early life experiences play a crucial role in shaping mental health. Adverse childhood experiences (ACEs) such as abuse, neglect, and household dysfunction are strongly linked to the development of mental health disorders later in life. Conversely, positive experiences, such as stable family relationships and supportive schooling, can foster resilience and healthy development.

Social Environment: Our interactions with others and our social connections significantly affect our mental health. Loneliness and social isolation can lead to depression and anxiety, while strong social support networks are protective against mental health issues. Positive relationships provide emotional support, reduce stress, and contribute to a sense of belonging and purpose.

Economic Factors: Socioeconomic status (SES) is closely linked to mental health. Individuals with lower SES are at higher risk of mental health problems due to factors such as financial stress, limited access to healthcare, and living in unsafe or unstable environments. Conversely, higher SES often affords better access to resources that support mental well-being, such as quality healthcare, education, and safe living conditions.

Physical Environment: The physical environment, including where we live and work, can also influence mental health. Exposure to natural light, green spaces, and clean air has been associated with improved mood and reduced stress. In contrast, living in areas with high pollution, noise, and overcrowding can contribute to anxiety, depression, and other mental health issues.

Implementing Environmental Strategies: To promote mental health, it is essential to create environments that support well-being. This can involve fostering positive relationships, ensuring safe and stable living conditions, and advocating for policies that address social determinants of mental health. Individuals can also seek out and create supportive environments, engage in community activities, and build networks that enhance social support.

Lifestyle Choices

Our daily habits and choices play a crucial role in maintaining mental health. Lifestyle factors such as diet, exercise, sleep, and substance use significantly influence our mental well-being.

Nutrition: A balanced diet rich in essential nutrients supports brain health and mental function. Foods high in omega-3 fatty acids, antioxidants, and vitamins can improve mood and cognitive function. Conversely, diets high in processed foods, sugar, and unhealthy fats are linked to increased risk of mental health disorders, including depression and anxiety.

Physical Activity: Regular exercise is one of the most effective ways to improve mental health. Physical activity increases the production of endorphins and other neurotransmitters that enhance mood and reduce stress. Exercise also promotes better sleep, boosts self-esteem, and provides a healthy outlet for frustration and anxiety.

Sleep: Quality sleep is essential for mental health. Sleep deprivation can impair cognitive function, increase irritability, and exacerbate symptoms of mental health disorders. Establishing a regular sleep routine, creating a restful sleep environment, and practicing good sleep hygiene are crucial for maintaining mental well-being.

Substance Use: The use of substances such as alcohol, nicotine, and recreational drugs can have significant effects on mental health. While some individuals may use substances to cope with stress or emotional pain, this can lead to dependency and exacerbate mental health problems. It is important to seek healthier coping mechanisms and, if necessary, professional help for substance use issues.

Mindfulness and Relaxation: Incorporating mindfulness practices and relaxation techniques into daily life can greatly benefit mental health. Practices such as meditation, yoga, deep breathing, and progressive muscle relaxation can reduce stress, enhance emotional regulation, and promote a sense of calm and well-being.

Implementing Healthy Lifestyle Choices: To optimize mental health, individuals can adopt and maintain healthy lifestyle habits. This involves prioritizing nutrition, engaging in regular physical activity, ensuring adequate sleep, avoiding substance abuse, and incorporating mindfulness practices into daily routines. Making small, incremental changes can lead to significant improvements in mental well-being over time.

Understanding the factors that influence mental health is essential for both prevention and intervention. By recognizing the roles of genetic predispositions, environmental influences, and lifestyle choices, we can take informed and proactive steps to enhance our mental well-being.

Implementing this knowledge involves a multifaceted approach: acknowledging genetic risks and seeking early interventions, creating supportive and nurturing environments, and making healthy lifestyle choices that promote mental health. This holistic strategy empowers individuals to take control of their mental health, leading to a more balanced and fulfilling life.

In the next chapter, we will explore practical strategies for maintaining and improving mental health, drawing on the insights gained from understanding these influencing factors. This journey towards better mental health is a continuous process of learning, adapting, and growing, with the ultimate goal of achieving mental well-being and resilience.

CHAPTER 5: STRATEGIES FOR MENTAL WELLBEING

Mindfulness And Meditation

Mindfulness and meditation are powerful tools for enhancing mental well-being. They cultivate a state of focused awareness on the present moment, fostering a sense of peace and balance that extends into everyday life.

Understanding Mindfulness: Mindfulness involves paying attention to the present moment without judgment. It means being aware of your thoughts, feelings, bodily sensations, and surrounding environment through a gentle, nurturing lens. Mindfulness can be practiced anywhere, at any time, by simply focusing on your breath or any other focal point to bring yourself into the present.

Benefits of Mindfulness: Research has shown that mindfulness can reduce stress, anxiety, and depression. It improves concentration, emotional regulation, and overall mental clarity. By breaking the cycle of automatic, negative thought patterns, mindfulness allows for more thoughtful and deliberate responses to life's challenges.

Practicing Mindfulness: Begin with short, daily sessions of 5-10 minutes, gradually increasing the duration as you become more comfortable. Find a quiet space, sit comfortably, and focus on your breath. Notice the sensation of the air entering and leaving your body. When your mind wanders, gently bring your focus back to your breath without judgment.

Understanding Meditation: Meditation is a more formal practice of mindfulness, often involving sitting quietly and focusing on a single point of reference, such as the breath, a mantra, or an image. There are various forms of meditation, including mindfulness meditation, loving-kindness meditation, and body scan meditation.

Benefits of Meditation: Like mindfulness, meditation offers a range of mental health benefits. It reduces stress, improves attention, decreases symptoms of anxiety and depression, and enhances self-awareness. Regular meditation practice can also increase feelings of calm and relaxation.

Practicing Meditation: Start with a simple breathing meditation. Sit in a comfortable position, close your eyes, and bring your attention to your breath. Notice each inhale and exhale, and if your mind starts to wander, gently redirect your focus to your breathing. Consistent practice, even for a few minutes a day, can yield significant benefits over time.

Physical Activity and Mental Health

Physical activity is not only beneficial for physical health but also has profound effects on mental well-being. Regular exercise can reduce symptoms of mental health disorders and enhance overall mood and energy levels.

The Link Between Exercise and Mental Health: Exercise stimulates the production of endorphins, the body's natural mood elevators. It also increases the levels of other neurotransmitters such as serotonin and dopamine, which are crucial for regulating mood. Moreover, exercise reduces levels of the body's stress hormones, such as adrenaline and cortisol.

Types of Physical Activity: Various forms of exercise can benefit mental health. Aerobic exercises, such as walking, running, cycling, and swimming, are particularly effective in reducing anxiety and depression. Strength training, yoga, and Pilates also promote mental well-being by improving body image, increasing energy levels, and fostering a sense of accomplishment.

Implementing Physical Activity: Incorporate physical activity into your daily routine. Aim for at least 30 minutes of moderate exercise most days of the week. Find activities you enjoy to make exercise a sustainable habit. It could be as simple as a daily walk, a weekend hike, or joining a local sports team. Remember, the goal is consistency rather than intensity.

Exercise as a Social Activity: Physical activity can also be a social event. Joining a group class, participating in team sports, or exercising with friends can enhance social connections and provide additional mental health benefits. Social interaction during physical activity can reduce feelings of loneliness and increase motivation.

Mind-Body Exercises: Activities like yoga and tai chi combine physical movement with mindfulness, offering both physical and mental health benefits. These practices improve flexibility, strength, and balance, while also promoting relaxation and mental clarity.

Nutrition and the Brain

What we eat profoundly impacts our mental health. The brain requires a variety of nutrients to function optimally, and a balanced diet can enhance cognitive function, mood, and energy levels.

Nutrients Essential for Mental Health: Certain nutrients are particularly important for brain health:

- **Omega-3 Fatty Acids:** Found in fish, flaxseeds, and walnuts, omega-3 fatty acids are crucial for brain function and have been linked to reduced symptoms of depression.
- **Antioxidants:** Foods rich in antioxidants, such as berries, dark chocolate, and leafy greens, protect brain cells from damage and reduce inflammation.
- **Vitamins and Minerals:** B vitamins, vitamin D, iron, magnesium, and zinc are essential for neurotransmitter production and overall brain health. Deficiencies in these nutrients can lead to mood disturbances and cognitive decline.
- **Protein:** Amino acids, the building blocks of protein, are necessary for the production of neurotransmitters. Including high-quality protein sources like lean meats, eggs, and legumes in your diet can support mental health.

The Gut-Brain Connection: The gut and brain are closely connected, with the gut microbiome playing a significant role in mental health. A healthy gut can improve mood and reduce anxiety and depression. Probiotics and prebiotics found in fermented foods like yogurt, kefir, sauerkraut, and fiber-rich foods like fruits, vegetables, and whole grains can support a healthy gut microbiome.

Dietary Patterns and Mental Health: Research suggests that certain dietary patterns are associated with better mental health outcomes. The Mediterranean diet, which is rich in fruits, vegetables, whole grains, nuts, seeds, and healthy fats, has been linked to a reduced risk of depression. Conversely, diets high in processed foods, sugars, and unhealthy fats are associated with increased mental health problems.

Implementing a Brain-Healthy Diet: To support mental well-being through nutrition, focus on a balanced, varied diet rich in whole foods. Plan meals that include a variety of fruits, vegetables, lean proteins, whole grains, and healthy fats. Avoid excessive consumption of processed foods, sugary snacks, and beverages. Hydration is also crucial, so drink plenty of water throughout the day.

Implementing Strategies for Mental Wellbeing

Implementing these strategies for mental well-being involves making consistent, mindful choices that support your mental health. Here are some practical steps to integrate mindfulness, physical activity, and nutrition into your daily life:

1. **Create a Routine:** Establish a daily routine that includes time for mindfulness or meditation, physical activity, and

balanced meals. Consistency is key to reaping the long-term benefits of these practices.
2. **Set Realistic Goals:** Start with small, achievable goals. For example, begin with a five-minute meditation, a short walk, or incorporating one additional serving of fruits and vegetables into your diet each day. Gradually build on these goals as you become more comfortable.
3. **Monitor Progress:** Keep track of your mental well-being by journaling your experiences, emotions, and any changes you notice. This can help you identify which strategies are most effective for you.
4. **Seek Support:** Share your goals with friends or family members who can offer encouragement and support. Consider joining groups or classes that focus on mindfulness, fitness, or healthy eating.
5. **Be Flexible:** Life can be unpredictable, and it's important to remain flexible and adapt your routines as needed. If you miss a day of meditation or exercise, don't be discouraged. Simply resume your practice the next day.
6. **Practice Self-Compassion:** Be kind to yourself as you implement these strategies. Mental well-being is a journey, and it's normal to encounter challenges along the way. Celebrate your progress and treat setbacks as opportunities for learning and growth.

By incorporating mindfulness, physical activity, and healthy nutrition into your lifestyle, you can significantly enhance your mental well-being. These practices not only improve mood and cognitive function but also build resilience against stress and mental health disorders. In the following chapters, we will explore the role of therapy and counseling in mental health, providing further insights and tools to support your journey towards mental well-being.

CHAPTER 6: THE ROLE OF THERAPY AND COUNSELING

Types Of Therapy

Therapy and counseling play vital roles in addressing mental health concerns and promoting overall well-being. Various therapeutic approaches are available, each with its unique methods and focus areas. Understanding these can help individuals choose the most suitable type of therapy for their needs.

Cognitive Behavioral Therapy (CBT): CBT is one of the most widely used forms of therapy. It focuses on identifying and changing negative thought patterns and behaviors. By challenging these patterns, individuals can develop healthier ways of thinking and acting, which can reduce symptoms of depression, anxiety, and other mental health disorders. CBT is typically structured and goal-oriented, involving specific techniques such as cognitive restructuring, behavioral activation, and exposure therapy.

Dialectical Behavior Therapy (DBT): Initially developed for treating borderline personality disorder, DBT combines CBT principles with mindfulness practices. It focuses on teaching skills in four key areas: mindfulness, distress tolerance, emotion regulation, and interpersonal effectiveness. DBT is particularly effective for individuals who experience intense emotions, self-harm, or suicidal behaviors.

Psychodynamic Therapy: Rooted in Freudian theory, psychodynamic therapy aims to explore unconscious processes and unresolved past conflicts that influence present behavior. By gaining insight into these underlying issues, individuals can better understand and resolve their current problems. This therapy often involves exploring childhood experiences and the therapeutic relationship itself.

Humanistic Therapy: Humanistic therapies, such as person-centered therapy and Gestalt therapy, emphasize self-exploration and personal growth. These approaches focus on the individual's capacity for self-healing and self-fulfillment. The therapist provides a supportive, non-judgmental environment that encourages clients to explore their feelings and take responsibility for their choices.

Existential Therapy: Existential therapy addresses fundamental human concerns such as meaning, choice, and mortality. It helps individuals confront and make sense of life's inherent uncertainties and challenges. By exploring existential issues, clients can find greater purpose and authenticity in their lives.

Family Therapy: Family therapy involves working with families to improve communication, resolve conflicts, and understand dynamics that contribute to mental health issues. This approach recognizes that individual problems often arise within the context of family relationships and that addressing these relationships can lead to significant improvements.

Group Therapy: Group therapy involves one or more therapists working with several individuals simultaneously. This format allows participants to share experiences, provide mutual support, and learn from each other. Group therapy can be particularly beneficial for those dealing with issues such as social anxiety, addiction, or grief.

Finding the Right Therapist

Finding the right therapist is crucial for effective treatment. The therapeutic relationship significantly influences the success of therapy, so it's important to choose a therapist who is a good fit for your needs and preferences.

Identify Your Needs: Start by identifying the specific issues you want to address in therapy. Consider whether you need help with anxiety, depression, relationship issues, trauma, or other concerns. Knowing your goals can help you find a therapist who specializes in the relevant areas.

Research Therapists: Look for therapists with the appropriate credentials, experience, and specialization. Online directories, professional organizations, and referrals from healthcare providers can be valuable resources. Reading reviews and testimonials can also provide insights into a therapist's approach and effectiveness.

Check Credentials: Ensure that the therapist is licensed and certified by the relevant professional bodies. Licensing requirements vary by region, but typically include advanced education, supervised training, and adherence to ethical standards.

Consider Therapy Format: Decide whether you prefer individual, couples, family, or group therapy. Each format has its advantages, and the best choice depends on your specific needs and circumstances.

Initial Consultation: Many therapists offer an initial consultation to determine if they are a good fit for you. Use this opportunity to ask about their therapeutic approach, experience with your specific issues, and what you can expect from the sessions. Pay attention to how comfortable you feel with the therapist and whether their style aligns with your preferences.

Evaluate Compatibility: The therapeutic relationship is built on trust, empathy, and collaboration. It's important to feel heard, respected, and understood by your therapist. If you don't feel comfortable with a therapist after a few sessions, don't hesitate to seek another professional. Therapy is a deeply personal process, and finding the right therapist can make a significant difference in your progress.

Self-Help vs. Professional Help

Self-help strategies and professional therapy both play important roles in mental health care. Understanding their respective benefits and limitations can help you make informed decisions about your mental health journey.

Self-Help Strategies:

- **Self-Help Books and Online Resources:** Many books, websites, and apps offer valuable information and techniques for managing mental health. These resources can provide practical tools for coping with stress, anxiety, depression, and other issues.
- **Support Groups:** Peer-led support groups offer a sense of community and shared experience. They can provide emotional support, practical advice, and a sense of belonging.
- **Mindfulness and Relaxation Techniques:** Practices such as meditation, deep breathing, and progressive muscle relaxation can reduce stress and improve emotional well-

being. These techniques can be easily integrated into daily routines.
- **Lifestyle Changes:** Implementing healthy lifestyle habits, such as regular exercise, balanced nutrition, adequate sleep, and social connections, can have a significant impact on mental health.

Benefits of Self-Help: Self-help strategies are often accessible, affordable, and flexible. They can be a great starting point for individuals who prefer to manage their mental health independently or who are unable to access professional therapy.

Limitations of Self-Help: While self-help can be effective for mild to moderate issues, it may not be sufficient for severe or complex mental health conditions. Self-help lacks the personalized guidance and support that professional therapy provides.

Professional Help:

- **Personalized Treatment:** Therapists tailor their approach to meet the unique needs of each client. They can provide specific techniques and strategies that are most effective for your situation.
- **Expert Guidance:** Therapists have extensive training and experience in diagnosing and treating mental health

disorders. They can offer insights and interventions that go beyond what self-help resources can provide.
- **Support and Accountability:** Regular therapy sessions provide ongoing support and accountability. Therapists can help you stay on track, navigate challenges, and adjust your strategies as needed.

Benefits of Professional Help: Professional therapy is particularly beneficial for individuals with severe, persistent, or complex mental health issues. It provides a structured, supportive environment where deeper issues can be explored and addressed.

Combining Self-Help and Professional Help: Many individuals find that a combination of self-help strategies and professional therapy is most effective. Self-help can complement therapy by reinforcing the skills and techniques learned in sessions. Discuss with your therapist how self-help resources can be integrated into your treatment plan.

Conclusion

Therapy and counseling are powerful tools for addressing mental health issues and promoting overall well-being. By understanding the different types of therapy, finding the right therapist, and balancing self-help with professional guidance, you can take proactive steps towards improving your mental health.

Implementing these strategies involves being open to seeking help, exploring various therapeutic options, and committing to the process of self-discovery and growth. Remember that mental health is a journey, and finding the right support can make all the difference in achieving lasting well-being.

In the following chapters, we will delve deeper into specific therapeutic techniques, self-care practices, and the importance of building a supportive community. These insights will further equip you with the knowledge and tools to navigate your mental health journey effectively.

CHAPTER 7: COPING MECHANISMS AND RESILIENCE

Stress Management Techniques

In our fast-paced world, stress is an almost inevitable part of life. However, effectively managing stress is crucial for maintaining mental well-being. By incorporating practical stress management techniques, individuals can navigate life's challenges more effectively and maintain a sense of balance.

Mindfulness and Relaxation: Mindfulness involves focusing on the present moment without judgment. Techniques such as deep breathing, progressive muscle relaxation, and guided imagery can help calm the mind and reduce stress. Taking just a few minutes each day to practice mindfulness can significantly lower stress levels and improve overall well-being.

Time Management: Effective time management can alleviate stress by helping individuals prioritize tasks and set realistic goals. Creating a daily schedule, breaking tasks into manageable steps, and avoiding procrastination can lead to a more organized and less stressful life. It's also important to build in time for relaxation and self-care.

Physical Activity: Regular exercise is a powerful stress reliever. Physical activity releases endorphins, the body's natural mood elevators, and helps reduce levels of the stress hormone cortisol. Whether it's a brisk walk, a yoga session, or a workout at the gym, incorporating regular physical activity into your routine can significantly reduce stress.

Social Support: Building a strong support network is essential for managing stress. Talking to friends, family, or a trusted counselor can provide emotional support and practical advice. Social interactions can also provide a sense of belonging and reduce feelings of isolation.

Hobbies and Leisure Activities: Engaging in activities that bring joy and relaxation can be an effective way to manage stress. Whether it's reading, gardening, painting, or playing a musical instrument, finding time for hobbies can provide a much-needed break from daily stressors.

Healthy Lifestyle Choices: Maintaining a healthy lifestyle can enhance your ability to cope with stress. This includes eating a balanced diet, getting enough sleep, and avoiding excessive consumption of caffeine and alcohol. Taking care of your physical health can have a positive impact on your mental health.

Building Emotional Resilience

Emotional resilience is the ability to adapt to stress, adversity, and challenging situations. Building resilience doesn't eliminate difficulties, but it helps individuals handle them more effectively and recover more quickly.

Positive Thinking: Cultivating a positive mindset is key to building resilience. This involves focusing on strengths, appreciating positive experiences, and maintaining an optimistic outlook. Positive thinking can enhance problem-solving abilities and increase motivation.

Self-Awareness: Developing self-awareness involves understanding your emotions, strengths, and weaknesses. This awareness allows you to recognize stress triggers and respond to them more effectively. Journaling, mindfulness, and therapy can help increase self-awareness.

Emotional Regulation: Learning to manage emotions in a healthy way is crucial for resilience. This includes recognizing and expressing emotions appropriately, as well as using techniques such as deep breathing, visualization, and mindfulness to calm the mind during stressful situations.

Adaptability: Being open to change and willing to adapt to new circumstances can enhance resilience. This involves being flexible in your thinking and approaches, and viewing challenges as opportunities for growth rather than threats.

Problem-Solving Skills: Developing strong problem-solving skills can help individuals navigate difficult situations more effectively. This involves identifying the problem, generating potential solutions, evaluating options, and taking decisive action.

Building Strong Relationships: Establishing and maintaining strong relationships provides emotional support and a sense of community. Positive relationships with friends, family, and colleagues can provide comfort and stability during times of stress.

Coping with Crisis and Trauma

Crisis and trauma can have profound impacts on mental health. Effective coping strategies are essential for navigating these difficult experiences and facilitating recovery.

Seeking Professional Help: In the aftermath of a crisis or trauma, seeking professional help is crucial. Therapists and counselors can provide specialized support and interventions to help individuals process their experiences and begin healing. Trauma-focused therapies, such as Eye Movement Desensitization and

Reprocessing (EMDR) and Trauma-Focused Cognitive Behavioral Therapy (TF-CBT), are particularly effective.

Self-Compassion: Practicing self-compassion involves being kind to yourself and recognizing that suffering and setbacks are part of the human experience. This approach encourages self-care and reduces feelings of shame and self-criticism.

Creating a Safe Environment: Ensuring physical and emotional safety is a priority after experiencing trauma. This might involve establishing boundaries, seeking out supportive relationships, and creating a stable and predictable routine.

Expressive Activities: Engaging in activities that allow for expression of emotions can be therapeutic. This might include writing, art, music, or other creative outlets. Expressive activities can help individuals process their experiences and gain a sense of control.

Grounding Techniques: Grounding techniques can help individuals stay connected to the present moment and reduce feelings of dissociation or overwhelm. Techniques such as deep breathing, progressive muscle relaxation, and focusing on sensory experiences can provide immediate relief during moments of distress.

Building a Support Network: Connecting with others who have experienced similar challenges can provide validation and support. Support groups, both in-person and online, offer a sense of community and shared understanding.

Implementing Coping Mechanisms and Building Resilience

Implementing effective coping mechanisms and building resilience requires consistent effort and practice. Here are some practical steps to help you integrate these strategies into your daily life:

1. **Set Realistic Goals:** Start by setting small, achievable goals related to stress management and resilience-building. Gradually increase the complexity and scope of these goals as you become more comfortable.
2. **Develop a Routine:** Establish a daily routine that includes time for stress management techniques, physical activity, and self-care. Consistency is key to making these practices a regular part of your life.
3. **Monitor Your Progress:** Keep track of your progress by journaling or using a tracking app. Note any improvements in your stress levels, emotional resilience, and overall well-being.
4. **Seek Feedback:** Share your goals and progress with a trusted friend, family member, or therapist. They can

provide encouragement, support, and constructive feedback.

5. **Stay Flexible:** Life is unpredictable, and it's important to remain flexible in your approach. If a particular strategy isn't working, be open to trying something new. Adaptability is a crucial component of resilience.
6. **Practice Self-Compassion:** Be kind to yourself throughout this process. Building resilience and developing effective coping mechanisms takes time and effort. Celebrate your successes, and don't be too hard on yourself when setbacks occur.

By incorporating these strategies into your life, you can enhance your ability to cope with stress, build emotional resilience, and navigate crises and trauma more effectively. These skills not only improve mental health but also contribute to a more balanced, fulfilling life.

In the following chapters, we will explore the importance of social connections, the role of creative expression, and the impact of spirituality on mental well-being. These insights will further equip you with the knowledge and tools to support your mental health journey.

CHAPTER 8: THE IMPACT OF RELATIONSHIPS

Healthy Relationships and Mental Health

Healthy relationships are foundational to mental well-being. They provide emotional support, create a sense of belonging, and contribute to overall happiness. Understanding the qualities that define healthy relationships can help individuals cultivate and maintain these essential connections.

Key Characteristics of Healthy Relationships:

- **Mutual Respect:** In healthy relationships, both parties respect each other's boundaries, values, and opinions. This respect fosters trust and reduces conflict.
- **Effective Communication:** Open and honest communication is critical. This involves active listening, expressing feelings and thoughts clearly, and being receptive to feedback.
- **Support and Encouragement:** Partners in a healthy relationship offer support and encouragement, helping each other grow and achieve personal goals.
- **Trust and Honesty:** Trust is built through consistent honesty and reliability. Trust allows individuals to feel safe and secure in their relationships.

- **Equality and Fairness:** Healthy relationships are balanced, with both parties having an equal say and contributing to decision-making processes.
- **Conflict Resolution:** Disagreements are inevitable, but how they are handled makes a difference. Healthy relationships involve resolving conflicts constructively and without hostility.

Benefits of Healthy Relationships:

- **Emotional Support:** Having someone to share your joys and sorrows with can alleviate stress and improve mental health.
- **Increased Happiness:** Positive interactions with loved ones release oxytocin and other "feel-good" hormones, enhancing mood and well-being.
- **Improved Self-Esteem:** Being valued and appreciated in a relationship boosts self-worth and confidence.
- **Enhanced Coping Skills:** Supportive relationships provide resources and perspectives that help individuals cope with life's challenges more effectively.
- **Physical Health Benefits:** Healthy relationships can also lead to better physical health, including lower blood pressure, improved immune function, and longer lifespan.

Dealing with Toxic Relationships

While healthy relationships enhance mental well-being, toxic relationships can have the opposite effect. Toxic relationships are characterized by behaviors that are emotionally, psychologically, or even physically damaging. Recognizing and addressing these relationships is crucial for protecting mental health.

Signs of a Toxic Relationship:

- **Constant Criticism:** Persistent negative feedback that undermines self-esteem and self-worth.
- **Manipulation:** Controlling behavior that seeks to dominate or exploit the other person.
- **Lack of Support:** Emotional neglect or indifference to the other person's needs and feelings.
- **Jealousy and Possessiveness:** Excessive jealousy and possessiveness that restrict personal freedom and autonomy.
- **Gaslighting:** Psychological manipulation that makes the other person question their reality and sanity.
- **Hostility:** Frequent arguments, insults, and hostility that create a hostile and unsafe environment.

Impact of Toxic Relationships on Mental Health:

- **Increased Stress and Anxiety:** The constant tension and conflict in toxic relationships can lead to chronic stress and anxiety.
- **Depression:** Feeling trapped or devalued in a toxic relationship can contribute to feelings of hopelessness and depression.
- **Low Self-Esteem:** Persistent criticism and manipulation can erode self-confidence and self-worth.
- **Isolation:** Toxic relationships often isolate individuals from other supportive connections, exacerbating feelings of loneliness and isolation.

Strategies for Dealing with Toxic Relationships:

- **Set Boundaries:** Clearly define what behaviors are unacceptable and communicate these boundaries firmly. Consistently enforce these boundaries to protect your well-being.
- **Seek Support:** Reach out to trusted friends, family members, or a therapist for support and guidance. External perspectives can help you see the situation more clearly.

- **Prioritize Self-Care:** Focus on self-care activities that promote your physical and mental health. This can include exercise, hobbies, and relaxation techniques.
- **Consider Professional Help:** Therapy can provide tools and strategies for managing toxic relationships and building healthier ones.
- **Evaluate the Relationship:** Assess whether the relationship can be improved or if it is necessary to distance yourself or end the relationship for your well-being.

Social Support Networks

Social support networks play a vital role in maintaining mental health. These networks consist of friends, family, colleagues, and other significant individuals who provide emotional, informational, and practical support.

Types of Social Support:

- **Emotional Support:** This includes empathy, care, and understanding from others, which can provide comfort and reassurance during difficult times.
- **Informational Support:** Advice, suggestions, and information from others can help individuals navigate challenges and make informed decisions.

- **Practical Support:** Tangible assistance, such as help with tasks, financial support, or providing transportation, can alleviate stress and improve well-being.
- **Companionship:** Spending time with others and engaging in social activities can reduce feelings of loneliness and enhance mood.

Building and Maintaining a Social Support Network:

- **Nurture Existing Relationships:** Invest time and effort in maintaining strong connections with friends and family. Regular communication and shared activities can strengthen these bonds.
- **Seek Out New Connections:** Join clubs, groups, or organizations that align with your interests and values. This can help you meet new people and expand your social network.
- **Be Open and Authentic:** Building genuine connections requires openness and authenticity. Share your thoughts and feelings honestly, and be receptive to others' experiences.
- **Offer Support:** Being a supportive friend or family member fosters reciprocity. When you provide support to others, they are more likely to offer support in return.

- **Engage in Community Activities:** Participating in community events and volunteering can create a sense of belonging and connect you with like-minded individuals.

Benefits of a Strong Social Support Network:

- **Emotional Well-Being:** Strong social connections can buffer against stress, reduce symptoms of anxiety and depression, and increase overall happiness.
- **Sense of Belonging:** Feeling connected to a community provides a sense of belonging and purpose.
- **Improved Coping Skills:** Social support provides resources and perspectives that help individuals manage challenges more effectively.
- **Enhanced Physical Health:** Socially connected individuals often experience better physical health outcomes, including lower rates of chronic illness and improved immune function.

Implementing Relationship Strategies

Implementing strategies to foster healthy relationships, manage toxic ones, and build robust social support networks involves deliberate and consistent effort.

Here are some practical steps:

1. **Assess Your Relationships:** Reflect on your current relationships and identify which ones are healthy, which may need improvement, and which might be toxic.
2. **Communicate Openly:** Practice open and honest communication with your loved ones. Express your needs, listen actively, and be willing to work through conflicts constructively.
3. **Set Healthy Boundaries:** Establish clear boundaries in your relationships to protect your mental and emotional well-being. Communicate these boundaries assertively and consistently.
4. **Prioritize Quality Over Quantity:** Focus on cultivating a few deep, meaningful relationships rather than spreading yourself too thin with numerous superficial connections.
5. **Engage in Mutual Support:** Offer support to your friends and family, and don't hesitate to seek support when you need it. Reciprocity strengthens relationships.
6. **Invest in Self-Care:** Take care of your own mental and emotional health, as this enables you to be a better friend, partner, or family member.

By fostering healthy relationships, addressing toxic ones, and building a supportive social network, you can significantly enhance your mental well-being. These strategies not only provide emotional support and resilience but also contribute to a richer, more fulfilling life.

In the following chapters, we will explore the role of creative expression, spirituality, and other holistic practices in mental health. These insights will further equip you with the knowledge and tools to support your mental health journey.

CHAPTER 9: MENTAL HEALTH IN DIFFERENT LIFE STAGES

Childhood And Adolescence

Mental health is a critical aspect of development from childhood through adolescence. During these formative years, experiences and relationships significantly shape an individual's emotional and psychological well-being. Understanding the mental health needs at each stage can help caregivers, educators, and mental health professionals provide appropriate support.

Mental Health in Childhood:

- **Emotional Development:** Children learn to identify and express their emotions. They develop coping mechanisms for dealing with both positive and negative feelings. Supportive environments encourage healthy emotional development.
- **Behavioral Patterns:** Childhood is when behavioral patterns are established. Consistent discipline, positive reinforcement, and clear boundaries help children develop self-control and positive behavior.
- **Social Skills:** Interaction with peers and adults teaches children social skills. Playtime, cooperative activities, and guided interactions promote social competence and empathy.
- **Cognitive Growth:** Mental health and cognitive development are intertwined. Positive mental health supports learning and

intellectual growth, while cognitive stimulation can enhance emotional well-being.

Challenges and Support Strategies in Childhood:

- **Early Signs of Disorders:** Identifying early signs of mental health disorders, such as anxiety, ADHD, or autism, is crucial. Early intervention can mitigate long-term effects and improve outcomes.
- **Parental Involvement:** Active parental involvement is essential. Open communication, emotional support, and engagement in the child's activities foster a secure attachment and emotional security.
- **Educational Environment:** Schools play a significant role. Mental health education, bullying prevention programs, and accessible counseling services create a supportive educational environment.
- **Play and Creativity:** Encouraging play and creative activities helps children express themselves and develop resilience. Creative outlets such as drawing, music, and imaginative play support emotional regulation.

Mental Health in Adolescence:

- **Identity Formation:** Adolescence is a time of identity exploration. Supportive environments allow teens to explore their interests, beliefs, and values safely.

- **Peer Influence:** Peer relationships become increasingly important. Positive peer interactions contribute to a sense of belonging, while negative influences can lead to risky behaviors and mental health issues.
- **Independence and Responsibility:** Adolescents seek independence and responsibility. Balancing autonomy with guidance helps teens develop decision-making skills and self-reliance.
- **Emotional Turbulence:** Hormonal changes and social pressures can lead to emotional instability. Teaching coping skills and providing emotional support can help teens navigate these challenges.

Challenges and Support Strategies in Adolescence:

- **Mental Health Disorders:** Depression, anxiety, eating disorders, and substance abuse are common in adolescence. Awareness and early intervention are key to addressing these issues.
- **Open Communication:** Maintaining open lines of communication with teens is vital. Encourage them to talk about their feelings and experiences without judgment.
- **Healthy Lifestyle Choices:** Promote healthy lifestyle choices, including regular physical activity, balanced nutrition, and adequate sleep. These habits support overall mental and physical health.

- **Mental Health Education:** Educating teens about mental health, stress management, and self-care empowers them to take charge of their well-being.

Adulthood

Adulthood brings new responsibilities and challenges that impact mental health. Understanding the unique needs of adults at different stages can help in providing appropriate support and interventions.

Mental Health in Early Adulthood:

- **Life Transitions:** Early adulthood involves significant life transitions, such as starting a career, forming intimate relationships, and possibly becoming a parent. These changes can be both exciting and stressful.
- **Career Development:** Job satisfaction and work-life balance are critical for mental health. Supportive workplaces that promote mental health awareness and provide resources for stress management contribute to well-being.
- **Relationships:** Romantic relationships and friendships continue to play a crucial role. Healthy relationships provide emotional support and stability, while unhealthy ones can lead to stress and mental health issues.

Challenges and Support Strategies in Early Adulthood:

- **Managing Stress:** Teaching stress management techniques, such as mindfulness, relaxation exercises, and time management, can help young adults cope with the pressures of adulthood.
- **Mental Health Resources:** Access to mental health resources, including therapy and counseling, is vital. Encourage seeking professional help when needed.
- **Building Resilience:** Fostering resilience through positive thinking, problem-solving skills, and a strong support network helps young adults navigate challenges effectively.

Mental Health in Middle Adulthood:

- **Work-Life Balance:** Balancing work, family, and personal life becomes more challenging in middle adulthood. Prioritizing self-care and setting boundaries are essential for maintaining mental health.
- **Health Concerns:** Physical health issues may arise, impacting mental health. Regular check-ups, a healthy lifestyle, and stress management are crucial.
- **Family Dynamics:** Parenting teenagers or caring for aging parents can be stressful. Support from family, friends, and professional services can alleviate some of these pressures.

Challenges and Support Strategies in Middle Adulthood:

- **Chronic Stress:** Chronic stress from career demands and family responsibilities can lead to burnout. Regular breaks, hobbies, and relaxation techniques are important for stress relief.

- **Social Connections:** Maintaining strong social connections helps mitigate feelings of isolation and loneliness. Engage in social activities, community involvement, and maintain friendships.
- **Professional Support:** Access to professional support, such as therapy or counseling, can provide guidance and coping strategies for managing life's complexities.

Aging and Mental Health

Mental health in older adults is influenced by a range of factors, including physical health, social connections, and life transitions. Understanding these factors can help in providing appropriate support and improving the quality of life for the elderly.

Mental Health in Older Adulthood:

- **Life Transitions:** Retirement, loss of loved ones, and changes in physical health are significant transitions that impact mental health. Adjusting to these changes can be challenging.
- **Cognitive Health:** Cognitive decline, including memory loss and dementia, can affect mental health. Early detection and intervention are crucial for managing these conditions.
- **Social Isolation:** Older adults may experience social isolation due to loss of friends, family, or mobility issues. Social connections are vital for emotional well-being.

Challenges and Support Strategies in Older Adulthood:

- **Addressing Loneliness:** Combat loneliness by encouraging participation in social activities, community groups, and maintaining regular contact with family and friends.
- **Promoting Physical Activity:** Regular physical activity can improve mood, increase energy levels, and enhance overall well-being. Tailor activities to individual abilities and preferences.
- **Mental Stimulation:** Engage in activities that stimulate the mind, such as puzzles, reading, or learning new skills. This can help maintain cognitive function and mental health.
- **Access to Healthcare:** Ensure older adults have access to comprehensive healthcare, including mental health services. Regular check-ups and timely treatment of physical and mental health issues are essential.
- **Emotional Support:** Provide emotional support through active listening, empathy, and companionship. Encourage older adults to express their feelings and seek help when needed.

Implementing Mental Health Strategies Across Life Stages

Supporting mental health across different life stages involves understanding the unique challenges and needs of each stage and providing appropriate interventions and resources.

1. **Early Intervention:** Identifying and addressing mental health issues early can prevent them from becoming more severe.

Regular screenings and awareness can facilitate early intervention.
2. **Education and Awareness:** Educating individuals about mental health, coping strategies, and available resources empowers them to take charge of their well-being.
3. **Holistic Approach:** Adopt a holistic approach that considers physical, emotional, social, and cognitive aspects of health. Encourage balanced lifestyles that promote overall well-being.
4. **Support Systems:** Build and maintain strong support systems, including family, friends, and community resources. Social connections are vital for mental health at all stages of life.
5. **Access to Services:** Ensure access to mental health services, including therapy, counseling, and support groups. Affordable and accessible services are crucial for effective mental health care.

By understanding and addressing the mental health needs at different life stages, individuals can lead healthier, more fulfilling lives. The strategies outlined in this chapter provide a framework for supporting mental well-being from childhood through old age, emphasizing the importance of early intervention, education, and a holistic approach to mental health.

CHAPTER 10: MODERN CHALLENGES TO MENTAL HEALTH

Technology And Mental Health

The rapid advancement of technology has transformed the way we live, work, and interact. While technology offers numerous benefits, it also presents unique challenges to mental health. Understanding the impact of technology on mental well-being is crucial in navigating the digital age.

The Double-Edged Sword of Social Media:

- **Positive Aspects:** Social media platforms can foster connections, provide support, and create communities for people with similar interests. They offer a space for self-expression and can be a source of inspiration and motivation.
- **Negative Aspects:** However, social media can also contribute to feelings of inadequacy, anxiety, and depression. The curated nature of online content often leads to unrealistic comparisons and a distorted view of reality.

Cyberbullying and Online Harassment:

- **Prevalence:** Cyberbullying is a significant issue, particularly among adolescents and young adults. The anonymity of the internet can embolden individuals to engage in harmful behaviors.
- **Impact:** Victims of cyberbullying often experience increased levels of anxiety, depression, and even suicidal thoughts. The pervasive nature of online harassment means that there is often no escape, exacerbating its impact.

Screen Time and Mental Health:

- **Sleep Disruption:** Excessive screen time, particularly before bed, can disrupt sleep patterns and reduce sleep quality, leading to fatigue and irritability.
- **Attention and Focus:** Constant notifications and the temptation to multitask can impair concentration and productivity, contributing to stress and mental fatigue.
- **Physical Health:** Prolonged screen time is associated with sedentary behavior, which can negatively impact physical health and, consequently, mental health.

Strategies for Managing Technology Use:

- **Set Boundaries:** Establish clear boundaries for technology use. Designate tech-free times, such as during meals or an hour before bedtime, to reduce screen time.

- **Digital Detox:** Periodically take breaks from digital devices to recharge and reconnect with the offline world.
- **Mindful Usage:** Be mindful of how and why you use technology. Focus on using it for meaningful interactions and limit time spent on activities that lead to negative emotions.
- **Promote Healthy Content:** Follow accounts and join communities that promote positivity and mental well-being. Unfollow or mute sources of stress or negativity.

Workplace Stress

The modern workplace is a significant source of stress for many individuals. High demands, long hours, and a lack of work-life balance can contribute to mental health issues. Addressing workplace stress is essential for maintaining overall well-being.

Sources of Workplace Stress:

- **High Workload:** Excessive workload and unrealistic deadlines can lead to chronic stress and burnout.
- **Job Insecurity:** Fears about job stability and career prospects can create anxiety and affect mental health.
- **Lack of Control:** Limited autonomy and decision-making power can contribute to feelings of helplessness and frustration.

- **Workplace Relationships:** Conflicts with colleagues or supervisors, as well as a lack of support, can negatively impact mental health.
- **Work-Life Balance:** Struggling to balance professional responsibilities with personal life can lead to stress and burnout.

Strategies for Managing Workplace Stress:

- **Time Management:** Prioritize tasks, set realistic goals, and break work into manageable chunks to reduce overwhelm.
- **Healthy Work Environment:** Advocate for a supportive and healthy work environment. This includes open communication, recognition of achievements, and access to mental health resources.
- **Self-Care Practices:** Incorporate self-care practices into your daily routine. This can include exercise, meditation, hobbies, and relaxation techniques.
- **Set Boundaries:** Establish clear boundaries between work and personal life. Avoid checking emails or working outside of designated hours whenever possible.
- **Seek Support:** Utilize available support systems, such as employee assistance programs, counseling services, and support groups.

Coping with Rapid Social Changes

The pace of social change has accelerated in recent years, driven by technological advancements, globalization, and cultural shifts. While change can be positive, it can also be a source of stress and uncertainty. Understanding how to cope with rapid social changes is essential for mental well-being.

The Nature of Rapid Social Changes:

- **Technological Advancements:** The constant evolution of technology impacts how we communicate, work, and live. Keeping up with these changes can be overwhelming.
- **Globalization:** Increased interconnectedness brings cultural diversity and new opportunities but also challenges related to identity and adaptation.
- **Cultural Shifts:** Societal values and norms are continuously evolving, affecting attitudes toward gender roles, relationships, and personal identity.

Impact on Mental Health:

- **Uncertainty and Anxiety:** Rapid changes can create feelings of uncertainty and anxiety about the future. Adapting to new norms and technologies requires constant learning and adjustment.

- **Identity and Belonging:** Navigating cultural shifts and global influences can impact one's sense of identity and belonging, leading to existential questions and stress.
- **Social Cohesion:** Changes in societal norms can affect social cohesion and relationships, creating generational gaps and conflicts.

Strategies for Coping with Rapid Social Changes:

- **Flexibility and Adaptability:** Cultivate a mindset of flexibility and adaptability. Embrace change as an opportunity for growth and learning.
- **Continuous Learning:** Stay informed and continuously educate yourself about new developments. This reduces fear of the unknown and enhances competence.
- **Community Engagement:** Engage with your community to build social support and a sense of belonging. Participate in local events, join groups, and connect with like-minded individuals.
- **Mindfulness and Reflection:** Practice mindfulness and reflection to stay grounded amidst change. This helps in processing emotions and maintaining mental clarity.
- **Professional Support:** Seek professional support if you find it challenging to cope with rapid changes. Therapists

and counselors can provide tools and strategies to manage stress and uncertainty.

Implementing Strategies for Modern Mental Health Challenges

Navigating modern mental health challenges requires a multifaceted approach that includes personal, professional, and community strategies.

1. **Personal Strategies:** Focus on self-care, mindfulness, and healthy boundaries. Regularly assess your technology use, manage workplace stress, and develop coping mechanisms for rapid social changes.
2. **Professional Support:** Utilize available mental health resources, such as therapy, counseling, and employee assistance programs. Professional guidance can provide tailored strategies for your unique situation.
3. **Community Engagement:** Build and maintain strong social networks. Engage with your community, participate in support groups, and foster meaningful connections.
4. **Education and Awareness:** Stay informed about the latest developments in technology, workplace dynamics, and societal changes. Knowledge empowers you to adapt and thrive amidst change.

5. **Advocacy:** Advocate for mental health awareness and support in your workplace, community, and online spaces. Promote policies and practices that prioritize mental well-being.

By understanding and addressing the modern challenges to mental health, individuals can enhance their resilience and well-being. The strategies outlined in this chapter provide a comprehensive framework for navigating the complexities of the digital age, workplace stress, and rapid social changes, empowering you to thrive in a constantly evolving world.

CHAPTER 11: CREATING A MENTAL HEALTH PLAN

Setting Mental Health Goals

Creating a mental health plan begins with setting clear, achievable goals. Just as with physical health, mental well-being requires intentional effort and consistent practices. Setting mental health goals provides direction and motivation, helping you to focus on what matters most for your mental well-being.

Identifying Personal Needs:

- **Self-Assessment:** Start with a self-assessment to understand your current mental health status. Reflect on your emotional state, stress levels, coping mechanisms, and overall satisfaction with life.
- **Identify Priorities:** Determine which areas of your mental health need the most attention. This could include managing stress, improving mood, enhancing relationships, or increasing resilience.
- **Set SMART Goals:** Ensure your goals are Specific, Measurable, Achievable, Relevant, and Time-bound. For example, instead of saying "reduce stress," set a goal like "practice meditation for 10 minutes daily to reduce stress over the next month."

Types of Mental Health Goals:

- **Short-Term Goals:** These are goals that you aim to achieve in the near future, typically within a few weeks to a few months. Examples include establishing a daily routine, improving sleep patterns, or starting a new hobby.
- **Long-Term Goals:** These goals focus on broader changes and take more time to achieve, such as building resilience, achieving work-life balance, or developing deeper, more meaningful relationships.

Examples of Mental Health Goals:

- **Daily Mindfulness:** Practice mindfulness or meditation for 10-15 minutes each day to reduce anxiety and increase present-moment awareness.
- **Physical Activity:** Engage in at least 30 minutes of physical activity, such as walking, jogging, or yoga, five times a week to boost mood and energy levels.
- **Social Connections:** Make a point to connect with friends or family at least twice a week to strengthen social support networks.
- **Self-Care:** Dedicate time each week to self-care activities, such as reading, taking a bath, or pursuing a hobby, to recharge and reduce stress.

Daily Practices for Mental Wellbeing

Implementing daily practices is essential for maintaining and improving mental health. Consistent routines and habits can significantly impact your overall well-being, helping you manage stress, boost mood, and enhance resilience.

Mindfulness and Meditation:

- **Mindfulness Practices:** Incorporate mindfulness practices into your daily routine. This can include mindful breathing, body scans, or mindful eating. Mindfulness helps increase self-awareness and reduces stress.
- **Meditation:** Regular meditation, even for just a few minutes a day, can calm the mind and improve emotional regulation. Use guided meditations or apps if you're new to the practice.

Physical Activity:

- **Exercise Routine:** Regular physical activity is crucial for mental health. Exercise releases endorphins, which can improve mood and reduce symptoms of depression and anxiety. Find an activity you enjoy, whether it's walking, dancing, cycling, or yoga.

- **Active Breaks:** Incorporate short, active breaks throughout your day, especially if you have a sedentary job. Stretch, take a quick walk, or do some light exercises to keep your body and mind active.

Nutrition and Hydration:

- **Balanced Diet:** Eat a balanced diet rich in fruits, vegetables, whole grains, lean proteins, and healthy fats. Nutrition plays a significant role in brain function and mood regulation.
- **Stay Hydrated:** Ensure you're drinking enough water throughout the day. Dehydration can affect concentration and mood, leading to feelings of fatigue and irritability.

Sleep Hygiene:

- **Consistent Schedule:** Maintain a consistent sleep schedule by going to bed and waking up at the same time each day, even on weekends.
- **Sleep Environment:** Create a sleep-conducive environment by keeping your bedroom dark, quiet, and cool. Avoid screens and stimulating activities before bedtime.

Stress Management:

- **Relaxation Techniques:** Practice relaxation techniques such as deep breathing, progressive muscle relaxation, or visualization to manage stress.
- **Hobbies and Interests:** Engage in activities that you enjoy and that provide a sense of accomplishment and joy. This could include reading, gardening, painting, or playing a musical instrument.

Social Interaction:

- **Build Connections:** Make an effort to build and maintain social connections. Spend time with friends, family, and loved ones. Join clubs, groups, or communities that align with your interests.
- **Communication:** Practice open and honest communication. Share your feelings and thoughts with trusted individuals, and be a good listener in return.

Monitoring Progress and Adjusting Strategies

Regularly monitoring your progress and adjusting your strategies is crucial for maintaining mental health and achieving your goals. Life is dynamic, and your mental health plan should be flexible enough to adapt to changing circumstances and needs.

Tracking Progress:

- **Journaling:** Keep a journal to record your thoughts, feelings, and experiences. Reflecting on your entries can help you identify patterns, triggers, and progress.
- **Mood Tracking:** Use a mood tracker app or a simple chart to monitor your mood daily. This can help you see trends and identify factors that influence your emotional state.
- **Goal Review:** Regularly review your goals and assess your progress. Celebrate small victories and recognize areas where you may need to put in more effort.

Evaluating Effectiveness:

- **Self-Reflection:** Take time to reflect on the effectiveness of the strategies you are using. Are they helping you achieve your goals? Do they make you feel better?
- **Feedback:** Seek feedback from trusted friends, family, or a mental health professional. They can provide insights and suggestions that you might not have considered.
- **Flexibility:** Be flexible in your approach. If a particular strategy isn't working, don't be afraid to adjust it or try something new.

Adjusting Strategies:

- **Modify Goals:** If you find your goals are too ambitious or too easy, adjust them to be more realistic and challenging. Your goals should evolve as you grow and progress.
- **Incorporate New Practices:** As you learn more about yourself and what works for you, incorporate new practices into your routine. This could include new relaxation techniques, different forms of exercise, or additional social activities.
- **Seek Professional Help:** If you are struggling to achieve your goals or manage your mental health, consider seeking professional help. Therapists and counselors can provide tailored strategies and support.

Sustaining Long-Term Wellbeing:

- **Consistency:** Consistency is key to maintaining mental health. Stick with your daily practices and make them a regular part of your life.
- **Adaptability:** Be adaptable and open to change. Life is unpredictable, and your mental health plan should be able to adapt to new challenges and circumstances.
- **Self-Compassion:** Practice self-compassion. Understand that setbacks are a natural part of the journey. Treat yourself with kindness and patience as you work towards your mental health goals.

Implementing a Mental Health Plan

Creating and implementing a mental health plan involves setting goals, establishing daily practices, and regularly monitoring and adjusting your strategies. By taking a proactive approach to your mental well-being, you can build resilience, manage stress, and enhance your overall quality of life.

1. **Set Clear Goals:** Identify your mental health needs and set SMART goals that are specific, measurable, achievable, relevant, and time-bound.
2. **Incorporate Daily Practices:** Implement daily practices such as mindfulness, physical activity, balanced nutrition, and social interaction to support your mental well-being.
3. **Monitor and Adjust:** Regularly track your progress, evaluate the effectiveness of your strategies, and make adjustments as needed. Be flexible and open to change.
4. **Seek Support:** Utilize available resources, including professional help, support groups, and social networks. Building a strong support system is crucial for long-term mental health.

By following these steps and continuously refining your approach, you can create a comprehensive and effective mental health plan that supports your well-being and helps you navigate the challenges of life.

CHAPTER 12: RESOURCES AND FURTHER READING

Books, Websites, And Organizations

Navigating the journey to mental wellness is enriched by accessing a variety of resources. Below are some highly recommended books, websites, and organizations that provide valuable information, support, and guidance for mental health.

Books:

- **"The Body Keeps the Score" by Bessel van der Kolk:** This seminal work explores the profound effects of trauma on the body and mind, offering insights into healing through various therapies.
- **"Mindfulness in Plain English" by Bhante Henepola Gunaratana:** A straightforward guide to mindfulness and meditation, providing practical advice for beginners and experienced practitioners alike.
- **"An Unquiet Mind" by Kay Redfield Jamison:** A powerful memoir detailing the author's experiences with bipolar disorder, blending personal narrative with professional insights.
- **"Lost Connections" by Johann Hari:** This book explores the root causes of depression and anxiety, challenging

conventional wisdom and offering new perspectives on mental health.
- **"Daring Greatly" by Brené Brown:** Brown's exploration of vulnerability, courage, and shame provides valuable lessons on how embracing our imperfections can lead to a more fulfilling life.

Websites:

- **National Institute of Mental Health (NIMH) [www.nimh.nih.gov]:** NIMH offers comprehensive information on mental disorders, treatment options, and current research. It's an excellent resource for understanding various mental health conditions.
- **Mental Health America (MHA) [www.mhanational.org]:** MHA provides a range of tools, resources, and support for individuals seeking to improve their mental health. Their website includes screening tools, educational materials, and links to local resources.
- **Psychology Today [www.psychologytoday.com]:** A robust platform featuring articles written by mental health professionals, a therapist directory, and various self-help resources.
- **Mind [www.mind.org.uk]:** A UK-based charity providing advice and support to empower anyone experiencing a

mental health problem. They offer information on mental health conditions, advice on getting help, and resources for advocacy.
- **Headspace [www.headspace.com]**: A popular app and website offering guided meditation and mindfulness exercises designed to reduce stress and improve mental well-being.

Organizations:

- **American Psychological Association (APA) [www.apa.org]**: The APA provides resources for understanding psychology, finding a psychologist, and accessing psychological research.
- **National Alliance on Mental Illness (NAMI) [www.nami.org]**: NAMI offers support, education, and advocacy for individuals and families affected by mental illness. They provide local support groups, educational programs, and advocacy initiatives.
- **World Health Organization (WHO) [www.who.int]**: WHO's mental health section offers global perspectives on mental health, including research, statistics, and policy recommendations.
- **Substance Abuse and Mental Health Services Administration (SAMHSA) [www.samhsa.gov]**:

SAMHSA provides information on mental health and substance use disorders, treatment options, and support services.
- **Crisis Text Line [www.crisistextline.org]:** A free, 24/7 support service for individuals in crisis. Text-based support is available by texting "HELLO" to 741741 in the United States.

Emergency Helplines and Support Groups

In times of crisis, knowing where to turn can make all the difference. Below are emergency helplines and support groups that offer immediate assistance and ongoing support for various mental health challenges.

Emergency Helplines:

- **National Suicide Prevention Lifeline (USA):** 1-800-273-TALK (8255) – Provides 24/7, free, and confidential support for people in distress, prevention, and crisis resources.
- **Samaritans (UK and Ireland):** 116 123 – Offers a safe place for you to talk anytime you like, in your own way, about whatever's getting to you.
- **Lifeline (Australia):** 13 11 14 – A national charity providing all Australians experiencing a personal crisis

with access to 24-hour crisis support and suicide prevention services.

- **Crisis Services Canada:** 1-833-456-4566 – Provides crisis support to individuals in need, including those who are at risk of suicide.
- **Kids Help Phone (Canada):** 1-800-668-6868 – A free, confidential support service for children and youth in Canada. Available 24/7 for any concerns.

Support Groups:

- **Depression and Bipolar Support Alliance (DBSA):** DBSA offers peer-led support groups for individuals living with depression or bipolar disorder, providing a sense of community and shared understanding.
- **Alcoholics Anonymous (AA):** AA provides support for individuals struggling with alcohol dependence. Meetings are held worldwide, offering a supportive community and recovery program.
- **Al-Anon/Alateen:** For friends and family members of problem drinkers, providing support and understanding in a group setting.
- **Anxiety and Depression Association of America (ADAA):** ADAA offers online support groups for

individuals dealing with anxiety, depression, and related disorders.
- **Eating Disorders Anonymous (EDA):** EDA provides a supportive environment for individuals struggling with eating disorders to share their experiences and support each other in recovery.

Utilizing Resources for Comprehensive Support

Accessing the right resources is crucial for managing mental health effectively. Here's how to make the most of the available resources:

Educate Yourself:

- **Read Widely:** Engage with books and articles that provide diverse perspectives on mental health. Education empowers you to make informed decisions about your well-being.
- **Stay Updated:** Follow reputable websites and organizations for the latest research, treatment options, and mental health trends. Knowledge is a powerful tool in managing mental health.

Seek Support:

- **Reach Out:** Don't hesitate to contact helplines or support groups when in need. Immediate support can be lifesaving during a crisis.
- **Join Groups:** Participate in support groups that resonate with your experiences. Sharing with others who understand your struggles can provide immense relief and motivation.

Professional Guidance:

- **Find a Therapist:** Use directories and resources to find a qualified therapist or counselor. Professional guidance is invaluable in navigating mental health challenges.
- **Utilize Services:** Take advantage of services offered by mental health organizations, including therapy, counseling, and educational programs.

Develop a Personal Plan:

- **Set Goals:** Use the information and strategies provided in this book to set personal mental health goals. A structured plan enhances your ability to achieve and maintain mental well-being.
- **Regular Review:** Continuously monitor your progress and adjust your strategies as needed. Flexibility and persistence are key to long-term success.

Conclusion

Creating a robust mental health plan involves leveraging a variety of resources and support systems. By educating yourself, seeking support, and utilizing professional guidance, you can develop a comprehensive approach to mental well-being. Remember, the journey to mental health is ongoing, and having a wealth of resources at your disposal ensures you are well-equipped to navigate any challenges that arise.

CONCLUSION: CONTINUING THE JOURNEY

Summarizing Key Points

As we reach the conclusion of our exploration into the human mind and the paths to mental well-being, it is essential to reflect on the journey we've taken together. This book has aimed to provide a comprehensive understanding of mental health, from its foundational concepts to practical strategies for maintaining and enhancing it. Let us revisit some of the key points we've discussed:

1. **Foundations of Mental Health:** Understanding mental health is the first step in taking control of it. Recognizing the mind-body connection and debunking common myths empowers us with the knowledge to pursue genuine well-being.
2. **The Science of the Brain:** Our exploration of brain structure, neurotransmitters, and neuroplasticity highlighted how intricately our mental health is tied to our brain's function. This knowledge underscores the importance of both mental and physical practices in maintaining health.
3. **Recognizing Mental Health Disorders:** Identifying and understanding various mental health disorders such as anxiety, mood, personality, and psychotic disorders is

crucial. Early recognition and intervention can make a significant difference in outcomes.

4. **Factors Influencing Mental Health:** Genetic predispositions, environmental factors, and lifestyle choices all play significant roles in shaping our mental health. Awareness of these factors allows for more targeted and effective strategies.

5. **Strategies for Mental Wellbeing:** Implementing daily practices such as mindfulness, physical activity, and proper nutrition can profoundly impact our mental health. Consistency in these practices builds a resilient foundation.

6. **The Role of Therapy and Counseling:** Understanding the different types of therapy and the importance of finding the right therapist can help in navigating mental health challenges. Both professional help and self-help play crucial roles.

7. **Coping Mechanisms and Resilience:** Stress management techniques, building emotional resilience, and effectively coping with crisis and trauma are vital skills for maintaining mental health in the face of adversity.

8. **The Impact of Relationships:** Healthy relationships are foundational to mental health. Learning to navigate toxic relationships and build strong social support networks is essential.

9. **Mental Health in Different Life Stages:** Each stage of life brings unique mental health challenges and needs. From childhood and adolescence to adulthood and aging, understanding these stages helps tailor our approach to mental health.

10. **Modern Challenges to Mental Health:** The impact of technology, workplace stress, and rapid social changes are modern challenges that require contemporary solutions and adaptability.

11. **Creating a Mental Health Plan:** Setting mental health goals, incorporating daily practices, and monitoring progress form the backbone of a personalized mental health strategy. Flexibility and persistence are key to long-term success.

12. **Resources and Further Reading:** Utilizing books, websites, organizations, and emergency helplines provides a robust support network. Continuing education and reaching out for help when needed are critical components of mental health maintenance.

Encouragement for Ongoing Mental Health Maintenance

As we conclude, it's important to recognize that the journey to mental well-being is ongoing. Mental health is not a destination but a continuous process of growth, adaptation, and self-discovery.

Here are some final thoughts to encourage and inspire you on your path:

Embrace Lifelong Learning:

The field of mental health is ever-evolving. Stay curious and keep learning about new research, therapies, and strategies. This not only equips you with better tools but also keeps you engaged in your mental health journey.

Practice Self-Compassion:

Be kind to yourself. Understand that setbacks are a natural part of life and growth. Treat yourself with the same compassion and understanding that you would offer to a friend.

Build and Maintain a Support System:

Surround yourself with supportive, understanding people. Whether it's friends, family, or support groups, having a network can provide strength and comfort during difficult times.

Stay Flexible and Adaptable:

Life is unpredictable, and so is the journey to mental well-being. Stay flexible in your approach and be willing to adjust your strategies as needed. What works today might need to be modified tomorrow.

Celebrate Progress:

Acknowledge and celebrate your achievements, no matter how small they may seem. Progress in mental health is often gradual and recognizing your successes can provide motivation to keep moving forward.

Seek Help When Needed:

Never hesitate to seek professional help if you're struggling. Therapists, counselors, and support organizations are there to help you navigate challenges and find the best path forward.

Conclusion

The pursuit of mental well-being is a deeply personal and transformative journey. By equipping yourself with knowledge, embracing practical strategies, and maintaining a proactive approach, you can significantly enhance your mental health. Remember, this journey is unique to you, and there is no one-size-fits-all solution. Be patient, stay committed, and keep striving for a balanced and fulfilling life.

As you continue on this path, may you find the resilience, strength, and peace that come with a healthy mind. Thank you for embarking on this journey with us, and may your efforts lead to lasting well-being and happiness.

Made in the USA
Middletown, DE
04 August 2024